C000180555

READING

OUR TOWN 1950-2001

Reading Evening Post

READING
OUR TOWN 1950-2001

HAROLD HILL

First published in Great Britain in 2001 by
The Breedon Books Publishing Company Limited
Breedon House, 3 The Parker Centre, Derby, DE21 4SZ.

ISBN 1 85983 275 X

Printed and bound by Butler & Tanner, Frome, Somerset, England.
Jacket printing by GreenShires, Leicester, England.

Contents

Acknowledgements

I wish to thank most sincerely the following people for their help in the preparation of this book.

My son Michael Hill who is responsible for nearly all the pictures from 1990 to 2001 and for his photographic skills in selecting the important and interesting places. Without his help it would have been difficult to complete this book.

Very sincere thanks go to my good friend Mrs Lauretta Cotton who spent endless hours in the preparation and sorting out from the thousands of photographs available, and also for the many cups of tea she made for me over the weeks.

Special thanks to the *Reading Evening Post* for the use of their archives, and the editor and staff of the promotions department for their patience with me.

To Mr John Madjeski and the staff at the Madjeski complex for their help in sorting out the pictures from their records and allowing me to use them in this book.

Also, the management of the Oracle shopping centre for the loan from their archives of pictures of the construction of Reading's finest shopping centre.

Mr Doug Noyes and readers of the *Evening Post* who have contributed pictures for this book.

My thanks to Indy Cotton for designing my web site, which is www.pickofthepast.co.uk.

Special Note

Whilst every effort has been made to get all dates accurate, if an error occurs I apologise for it.

Introduction

Welcome to the second of Harold Hill's books. The first – *Images of Reading* – remains an excellent pictorial record of the town's history. Now with this book, the recent history of Reading from 1950 to 2001 is revealed.

Harold will take you travelling through the halcyon days of the 1950s when pub outings were popular and the town was still being rebuilt after the destruction of World War Two.

He'll take you on to the 1960s and '70s when many old houses and cottages were demolished to make way for 'arcade shopping', when the Palace Theatre was still thriving and through the political protests of the 1970s.

The 1980s saw Broad Street become pedestrianised, many buildings and shops had facelifts and small cinemas still prospered.

The last decade of the century saw two huge landmarks change the face of the town completely – The Oracle shopping centre and Madjeski Stadium. Step-by-step you can watch how these two vast structures went up to become milestones in Reading's history.

Each day in the *Evening Post* you can read Harold's trips back in time in Pick of the Past.

Reading: Our Town 1950-2001 gathers together times past in one volume for anyone who is interested in what will surely be the last days of Reading as a town, before it transforms into a grand city.

Andy Murrill
Editor
Reading Evening Post

The 1950s

In the years after World War Two, Reading welcomed many visitors from Europe. In 1948, this group of Dutch children joined Reading children before going on to camp at Boxford Common.

In the 1950s and 1960s stallholders still used the old Butter Market on Saturdays.

The old Reading Railway station in the 1950s. Note the advertising boards for Huntley & Palmers biscuits and Heelas Department store, now part of John Lewis Group.

Reading southern station in the 1950s.

How primitive were some of the vehicles that were used on important jobs, such as this Reading Borough Council drain cleaning lorry.

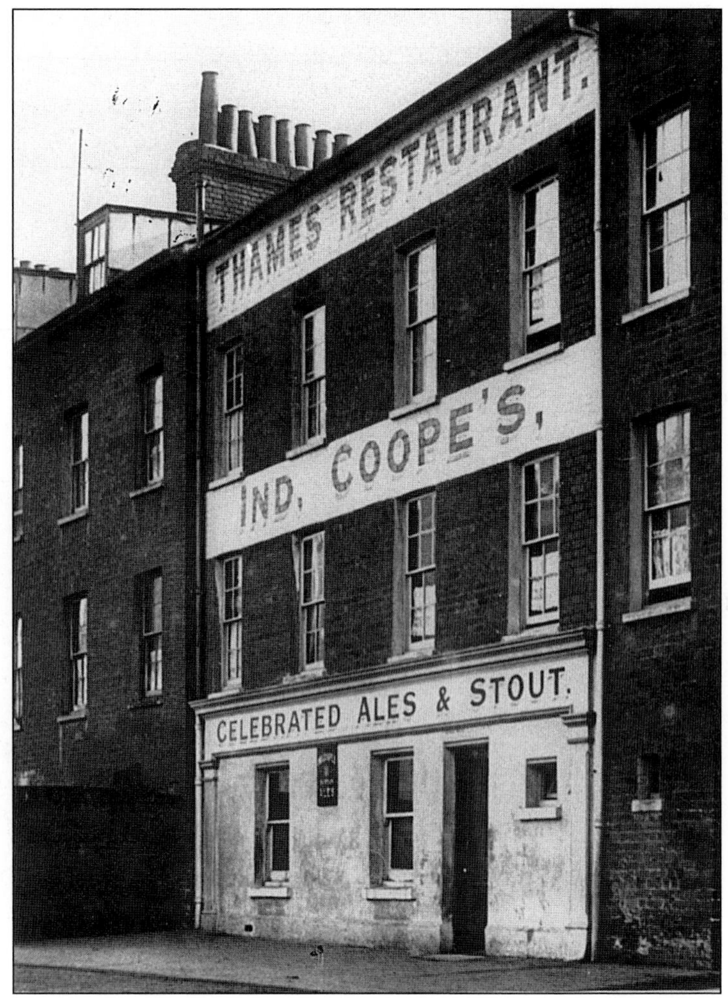

It was nice to take a stroll along the towpath of the River Kennet and the River Thames. Along the river frontage, there were many small pubs such as the Thames Restaurant.

Another favourite pub in the area known as Newtown was Leopold beer house which was a few yards from the small and friendly fishermen's pub called the Angler's Arms.

Pub outings were all the fashion in the 1950s. This group was on an outing to the seaside from Thames public house in Albert Road in Newtown.

This group of people from central Reading were off to enjoy a day at the seaside in one of Smith's luxury coaches.

In the 1950s, one of the main newspapers in Reading was the *Reading Standard*. This group from the print works was on the annual outing.

St Mary's Butts, which has undergone major changes in recent years, is pictured here in the 1950s.

The unchanging view of the Abbey Gateway as it looks out across the Forbury Gardens. All around it over the past 40 years, buildings have been knocked down and new ones built, but the Abbey Gateway never changes.

Older readers will remember the days of fogs and smogs in Reading. They were largely caused by smoke from chimneys, like these off the Oxford Road.

Reading Tradesmen and the Iris Ladies Rowing Club join forces to hold a dance at the Oxford Ballrooms in Reading.

A gathering of conductors and drivers of Reading Corporation Transport. Nearly all these men had served RCT faithfully throughout the war years, keeping the buses running often in terrible conditions.

The 1950s saw the rebuilding of bomb sites in Reading. Here is the construction of offices and shops on the bomb site opposite St Laurence's Church.

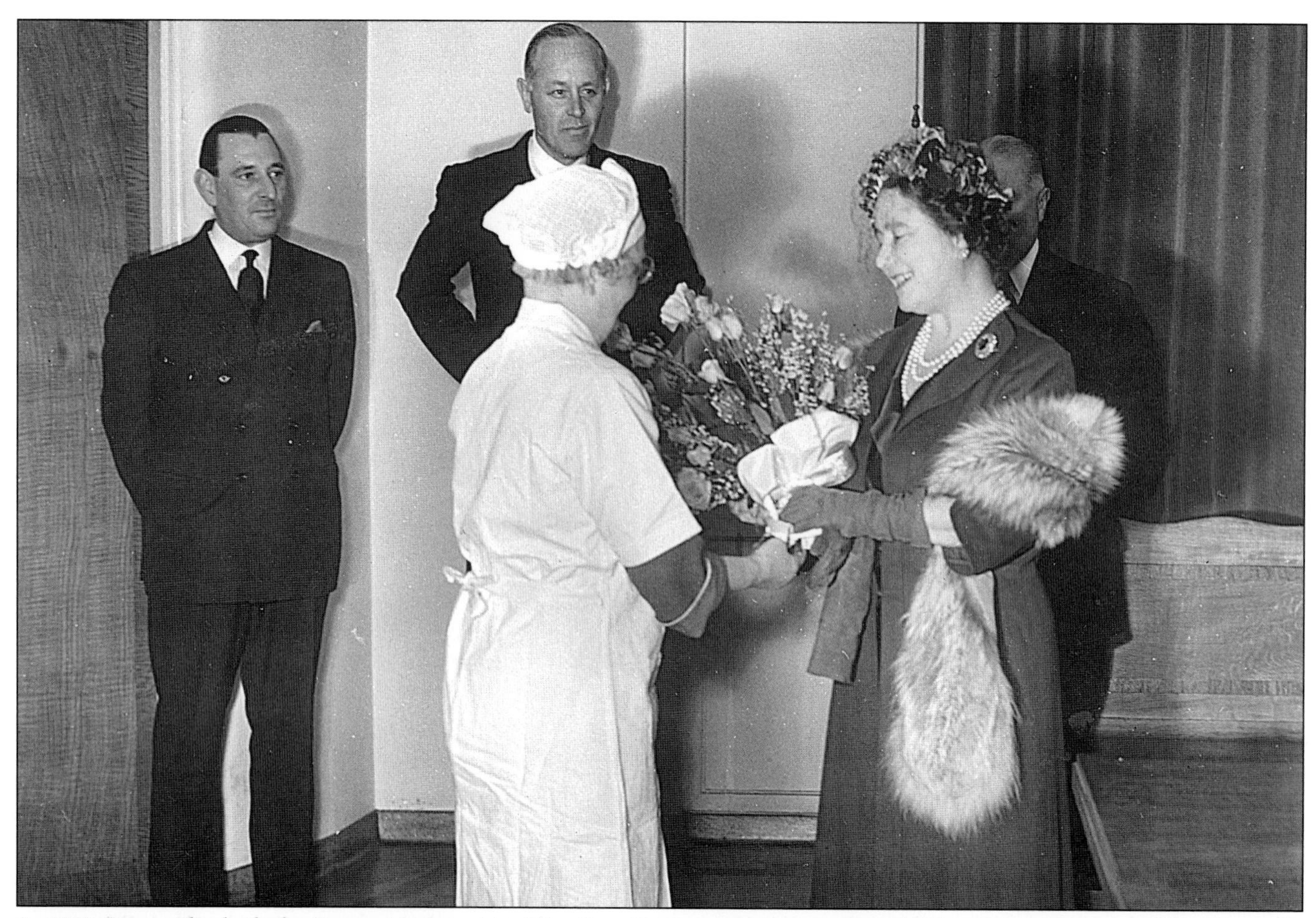

In 1955 Queen Elizabeth the Queen Mother visited Reading. She is seen here accompanied by the Mayor, Councillor Alf Smith, and also receiving a bouquet of flowers. She visited the Huntley & Palmers biscuit factory.

The Queen Mother with the Mayor, Councillor Alf Smith, and Mr H.R.H. Palmer MC, DL, chairman of Huntley & Palmers.

One of the centres of industry up until the end of the 1950s was the Caversham Mill which had ceased as a flour mill some 30 years previously, and which, until its closure in the late 1960s, was used as a mill for manufacturing cork.

Fifty years ago the motor car was used much less than today, but even in a wide road like Broad Street there was the occasional accident such as this one, when the driver lost control and hit a lamp standard outside Heelas flower shop.

Many of those who remember the 1950s would have had cause to use the casualty department at Battle Hospital. Here we see where casualties were admitted before the casualty unit was closed down and facilities moved to the Royal Berkshire Hospital in London Road.

When it opened its first building in Whiteknights Park in 1957, Reading University marked the beginning of a period of expansion.

One of the major means of transport in this period was the trolley bus system that served Reading so well for so many years. When the author was a trolley bus driver he drove the one you see here, number 176, in Broad Street in the 1950s.

Reading had another very efficient bus service that served the outlying country areas up until the 1970s. Here you see a Thames Valley single-decker.

This type of bus served the smaller routes that were just inside the borough boundary, like Woodcote Road.

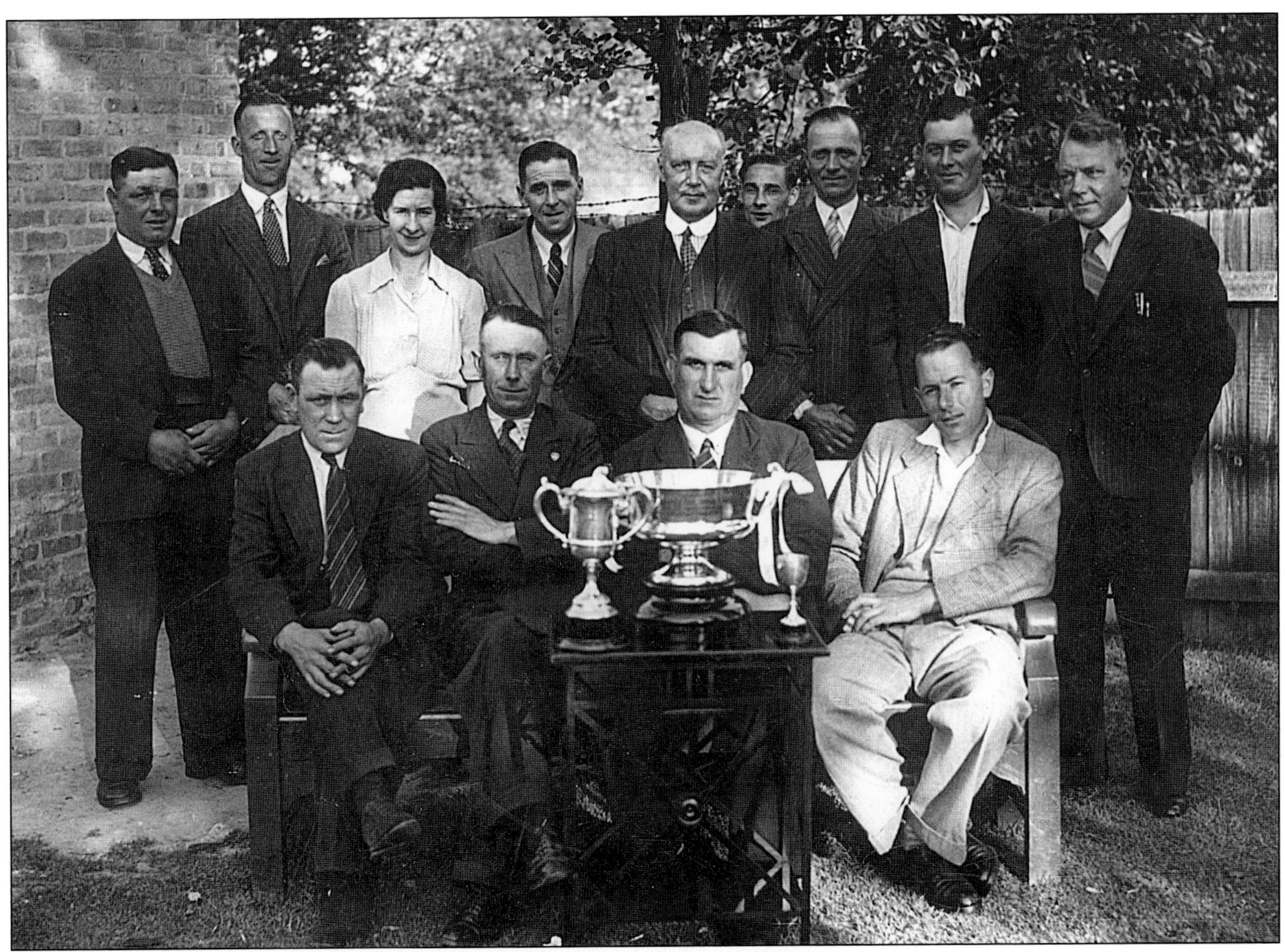

The 1940s and 1950s saw particular interest in darts. This photograph shows the team from the Prince of Wales which won a local darts league in 1947.

Battle Athletic are pictured at Elm Park, probably in the late 1950s or early 1960s.

The 1960s

Until 1999 the *Reading Evening Post* had a sister newspaper, the *Reading Standard.* To pay tribute to this much-loved paper here is a photograph of some of the members of staff from the *Standard.*

The typesetting room of the old *Reading Standard.*

In 1960, new printing press at the *Reading Standard* were installed. Here the National Dairy Queen (Miss M. Watson) is about to press the button to start up the new press.

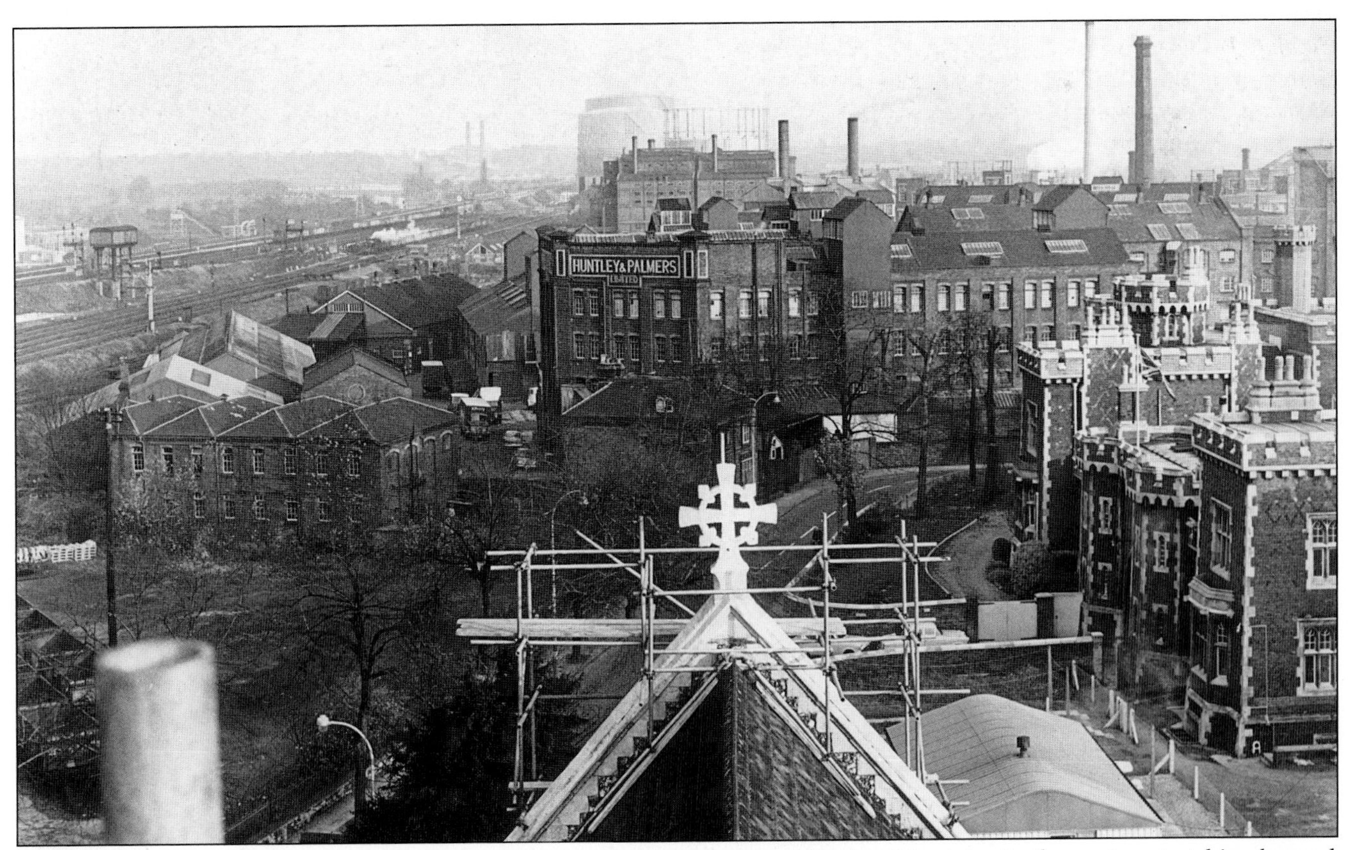

This aerial view, taken from the top of St James's Church, shows to the right the old prison. In the centre, stretching beyond almost to the gas works, was Huntley & Palmers biscuit factory. To the left is the main Western Railway line from Reading to Paddington.

This aerial view shows the vast size of Huntley & Palmers. The impressive front offices dominated the main part of the King's Road. Bottom centre is the River Kennet. Huntley and Palmers was not only the largest employer in Reading but once the largest biscuit maker in the world. The company began in 1822 but has now long since departed Reading in the late 1960s-early 1970s.

This view of central Reading shows the River Kennet flowing along at the back of the bus depot. In the centre is the Yield Hall car park; bottom centre are King's Road and Jackson's Corner; to the right the George Hotel and Minster Street.

Looking down on the Forbury Gardens with the lion and the bandstand bottom centre, to the left the fountain. In the centre is the Abbey Gateway and Shire Hall and Law Courts. To the right – and the largest building – was the Prudential offices, now demolished.

In the 1960s, the old Battle Hospital was undergoing major changes with alterations to the outpatients' department. Not very far away was the development of the new Battle Hospital, called the Abbey Block.

Dellwood Maternity Hospital was the subject of a major redevelopment in the 1960s, to help cope with Reading's growing birth rate. A new wing was built on and it still serves as a community hospital today.

A further example of the amount of building that was going on in Reading in the 1960s was the new multi-storey office block at Crown Bridge. To build this, developers first had to clear the old timber yard which was used as a car park until redevelopment.

The development of Kennet House under construction, with the White Lion pub in the centre.

In the 1960s the White Lion was rebuilt. This view is looking at the River Kennet across to Kennet House.

Kennet House in King's Road housed the treasury, surveying and property departments of Reading Borough Council which in later years were moved to the new Shire Hall.

The completed Kennet House and the old terraced houses just a short distance along the road and opposite the River Kennet. These terraced houses served the community faithfully for many years but their days were numbered.

A little further up King's Road, past Huntley and Palmers, is the Salvation Army's East Reading Branch which is dwarfed by the newly-built Norman Insurance building. This has recently been pulled down for further redevelopment.

Castle Street and St Mary's Church was an area that was untouched by the developers for some more years. These empty buildings were soon snapped up by various small businesses and the church has gone from strength to strength.

One of the sights that always caught the eye was that of the large beer tankers leaving on their journey to the Continent with Simonds Pale Ale on board.

One of the biggest major developments in the town in the 1960s – the clearance for the shopping centre now called Broad Street Mall but originally known as the Butts Centre. A large section of the town had to be cleared to accommodate this new shopping area.

Not only did Reading's town planners have to think of the growing demand for office space but also for housing. One answer was the multi-storey flats at Coley.

King's Road was particularly affected with this new development going up in Kennet Side.

The old barns at Southcote were demolished to make way for the Southcote Estate which was started in the late 1950s but not completed until the 1960s.

These flats were built for the people of Southcote with a good view of Prospect Park opposite. They still stand today.

The old and new with the erection of the Prudential building in the Forbury, outlined here against the famous Shire Hall, then the headquarters of Berkshire County Council. The Prudential building has now been pulled down.

One of the most popular arcades in Reading went from Broad Street to Friar Street. At the Broad Street end was the Reading Corporation parcels depot from where parcels were delivered by young boys on special bicycles. In the late 1950s and early 1960s this was altered by an insurance company and became known as the Bristol and West Arcade.

Trolley bus No 181 en route for Caversham Bridge, followed by one of the motor buses on its way to Donkin Hill.

Another of the smaller trolley buses, in the Whitley area outside the well-known Cecil's Transport Café.

Reading had another major bus company until the 1970s, the Thames Valley Bus Company, which covered the outlying villages.

A double-decker bus in Station Square, belonging to the Thames Valley Bus Company. These used to travel as far as the city of Oxford.

The third major bus company in Reading was privately owned by Mr Alf Smith and was known, not surprisingly, as Smith's Coaches. Here is one of about 70 in his fleet of luxury coaches.

27 November 1965 was a sad day for railway enthusiasts in Reading and indeed the country. Here we see the last steam train loco, No 7029 *Clun Castle*, as it thundered with its whistle blowing. The young boy with the imitation pistol is pretending to be one of the Great Train Robbers.

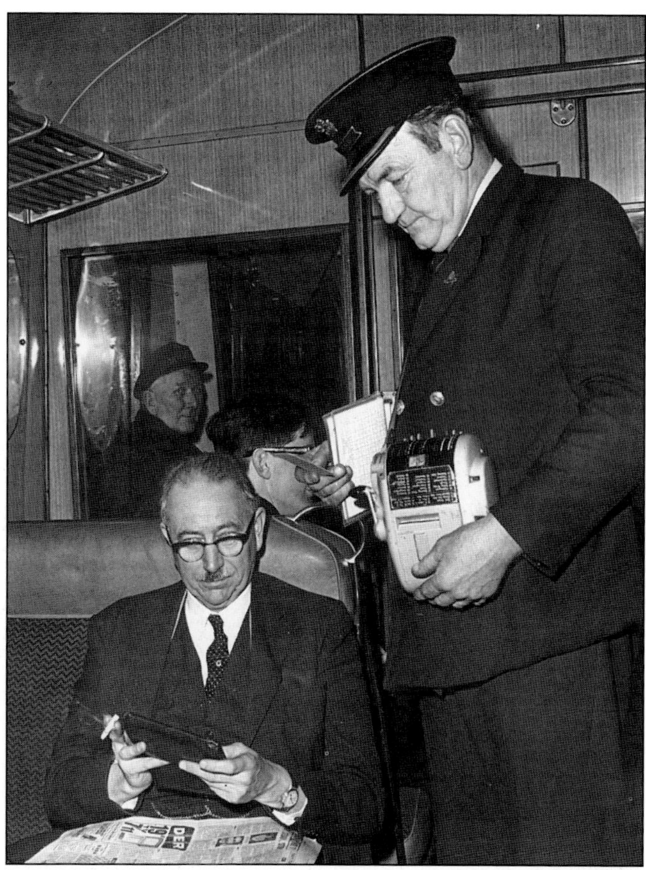

In January 1965 a pay-on-the-train system was introduced between Twyford and Henley. Here, one of the new conductors issues a ticket to a passenger.

June 1966 saw the final demolition of the Reading southern railway station which had served the southern part of the country for nearly 100 years. It was demolished in order to make way for a combined western and southern station.

In 1967 the old Southern Region combined with the Western Region of British Railways which used Reading General Station. The old Southern Region terminus was turned into a car park. This picture was taken from the top of the Western Region office block.

The steam trains were replaced by these ugly diesel-electric locomotives. Here at Reading station is the 10.42am to South Wales, with a goods locomotive running alongside.

The Oxford Road site before all the shops were pulled down to build what is now the Broad Street Mall. These shops went up as far as the White Hart Hotel on the corner of The Butts.

The completion of the Prudential building by the Forbury. What a vast building it was. Now, of course, it is gone to make way for more offices. This picture was taken from Abbots Walk.

The contrast of the British Rail Western Tower in Station Hill to the old derelict cottages in Greyfriars Road being demolished.

The demolition of the famous Blagrave buildings in Friar Street to make way for the C & A arcade and store. These flats were nearly a century old.

Friar Street was totally demolished from Cross Street to the Market Place in order to build the Prudential offices. This picture, taken by a photographer from the old *Reading Standard*, shows a panoramic view.

For more than 80 years a bridge of iron has spanned Reading's Vastern Road, carrying trains day and night. In August 1966 extensive work was carried out on this bridge and the rebuilding of it.

Thursday, 17 August 1967 saw a large power cut in central Reading and Caversham when a huge power cable blew up in the station yard. Emergency power generators were immediately put into action to power the biggest railway control box in Europe and rush hour trains were not affected.

March 1968 saw the opening of the multi-story Western Towers on Station Hill. In future this was to be the central 'nerve point' for trains in the Western and Southern Regions.

A splendid view taken by an *Evening Post* photographer from the top of Huntley, Boorne and Stevens and showing the skyline of Reading looking across the town centre with Letcombe Street in the foreground. Way in the background can be seen the Station Tower.

Oxford Road before the building of Broad Street Mall. On the left, on the corner of Cork Street, is the well-known clothing store, Langstons. On the far corner is the Foresters pub used by the actors from the nearby Palace Theatre.

In the 1960s, Reading was also in need of new entertainment venues and the Top Rank Suite was built in Station Hill. It is still there today, now a large bingo hall. Underneath this was the bus depot.

The major development for the University of Reading was its expansion into the beautiful Whiteknights Park. The old Whiteknights House is silhouetted against one of the modern halls of learning. The lovely lawns are still there.

View of Bridge Street looking through the offices of H. & G. Simonds brewery. At this time building work had already started on the bridge and on the demolition of the houses on the left.

For almost 100 years Spring Gardens, at the top of Whitley Street, comprised small shops and terraced houses. This picture was taken in 1967.

St Mary's Butts and the junction of Hosier Street where some of the oldest buildings in Reading once stood. This 1969 picture shows the Rediffusion television shop originally started by Herbert and Lascelles.

Mill Lane, now part of the Oracle shopping centre, with the old bus garages on the left. There was a furniture shop on the corner with Brennan's army surplus store next to it.

Practically all the houses and shops in this picture of Southampton Street have now been pulled down and replaced with new flats.

The Crown Hotel at the top of London Street, now redeveloped.

The famous Huntley, Boorne and Stevens biscuit factory which moved to Woodley in the 1970s.

Right up until 1968, Reading was famous for its brickworks and potteries, but like many other smaller firms they could not keep up with demand and developers bought the land which is now known as the Potteries Housing Estate.

Bridge Street towards St Mary's Butts. Photographs later in this book show the vast alterations which have taken place in this area.

Caversham saw the demolition of many old houses and cottages in the 1960s and the birth of a number of small shops and the new St Martin's Arcade at Caversham.

The closure of the *Reading Standard* offices and printing works in Valpy Street. This paper was later taken over by the *Reading Evening Post.*

Chatham Street car park towers above the Prince of Wales public house. This car park, built in the 1960s, is still going strong today.

Construction work on the Bath Road Bridge at Twyford which replaced the one that spanned the railway for over 100 years.

Major repairs and alterations to Skew Bridge on the Pangbourne-Oxford road, a main artery bridge.

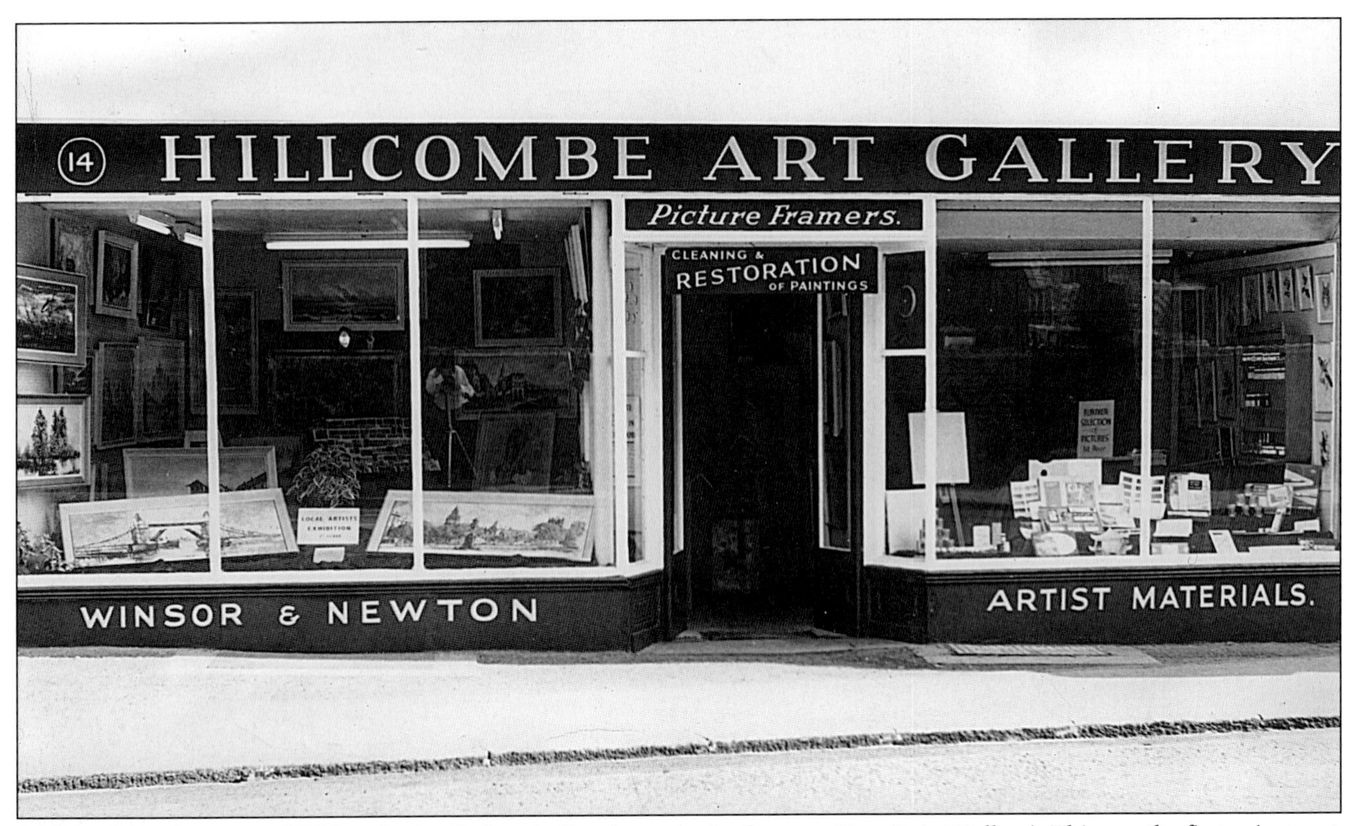

In 1960 the author opened Hillcombe Art Gallery in Gun Street (today know as Gun Street Gallery). This was the first private art gallery and picture framers in Reading to be opened after the war. The author later ran a fleet of mobile art galleries across the country.

Brock Barracks which served as home not only for the Royal Berkshire Regiment for so many years but also for other regiments during World War Two. The front of the barracks is still there today, but now there is a new housing estate behind it.

Whilst Brock Barracks is not now used as a military barracks, part of it is used as a Territorial Army drill hall. Here you see the opening ceremony when the regimental plate was on display on 16 June 1961.

The Territorial Army unit No 3 Stores Company RAOC threw its doors open to the general public at the TA Centre in Tilehurst Road in Reading on 3 March 1964.

In 1965 Britain was in the grip of the so-called Cold War, so it was interesting and challenging for these young children to visit a nuclear rocket and an anti-aircraft gun in Prospect Park, displayed by the 24 Missile Regiment of the Royal Artillery.

Military parades were all the craze in Reading, during the 1960s. Here, men and women of the Royal Air Force commemorate the Battle of Britain, marching down Broad Street.

1967 saw another march past of the Territorial Army as they paraded down London Street to take the salute outside the Town Hall.

Until the late 1960s, Reading had always been a military town. This picture shows the laying up of the colours of the 4/6 Royal Berkshire Regiment on 18 March 1967.

The Forbury Lion has its head averted as Major, the Honorable David Smith, Lord Lieutenant of Berkshire, inspects some of the men at the final parade of the county regiment.

The 1960s was the decade of demonstration and here a demonstrator has daubed their own protest against war on the window of the Army Information Centre in St Mary's Butts.

The military tradition of Reading also extends to the small village of Pangbourne and its Royal Naval College. The college's drum and fife band lead a procession of members of the Royal British Legion to Pangbourne Church for the lowering of the colours.

One of the leading schools in Reading has been Westwood School where not only the general and essential subjects are taught but also all forms of domestic work that students may have to face when they leave home.

Another leading school in Reading has been E.P. Collier where all sorts of events have been organised by teachers to bring interest and amusement to the children. Here, the Mayor of Reading is judging a fancy dress competition.

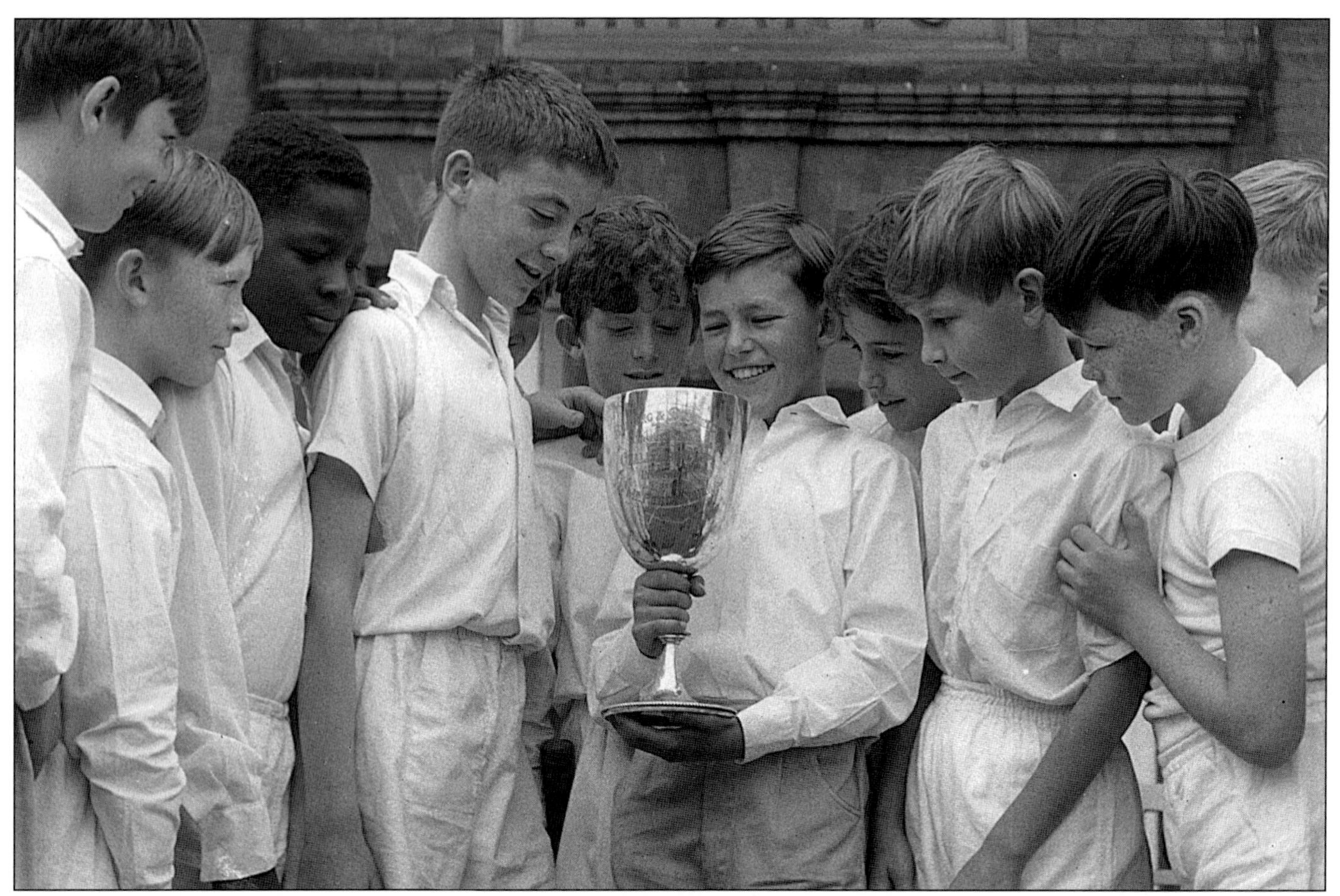

E.P. Collier School has always had a good sports base. This 1966 picture shows the school cricket team with the Reading and District Primary Schools Cricket Trophy they had just won.

1969 saw a grand opportunity for the children of the Saturday Club in Tilehurst to show their skills to a top referee Mr Fred Grace, who in turn passes on his knowledge of the game to the children.

Reading schoolchildren went up to see the *Nutcracker Suite* performed at the Royal Festival Hall.

In 1966, local man Mr W. Harder completed 40 years' service with the Automobile Association. Note his AA motorcycle in the background.

The years 1966 also saw the AA play an expanding role from their headquarters in London Road. Their new fleet of Mini vans is being inspected by the area manager, Mr R. Thomson.

Over 30 years ago, if you belonged to the AA you were given a rather smart badge, and if you displayed it on your car you received an equally smart salute from any passing AA man.

In 1967 Reading greeted Herr Bruno Recht, Burgermaster of Düsseldorf, when he brought over a girls' youth choir to sing to the citizens of Reading. Here they are pictured at the Civic Offices.

16 March 1968 saw the closure of an institution in Reading which had opened in 1890. It was the Thorn Street Register Office, and during its nearly 80 years some 30,000 couples had been married there. The registrar for many years was the perhaps inappropriately-named Mr W. Church.

Reading is famous for its prison in the Forbury Road. This is not a jail break but workmen demolishing the Victorian turrets which, right up until 1957, were used as living quarters for prison staff. This picture, taken in 1969, shows the start of a modernisation programme.

When men landed on the Moon in 1969, two copies of the *Evening Post* recording the epic event were sunk for posterity in concrete at the Council's Manor Farm sewage works.

Stop and search was the order of the day on 23 July 1969 when a prisoner, thought to have escaped from Reading Prison the day before, was found hiding in a turret inside the prison.

Square dancing in and around Reading is as popular today as it was over 30 years ago, when this picture was taken outside the George Hotel in Pangbourne.

The Kennet Morris Men give another of their outstanding displays at a fête in Burghfield in July 1966. Wherever the Morris Men go they are always greatly appreciated.

One of the popular things to do in the 1960s was to hold a tramps' dinner. Not only were they fun but it was a good way of raising money. Here is such an event being organised by the Earley Social Club.

The 1970s

The Jolly Porter in the railway station area, at the junction of Station Road with Vincent's Garage on the right and Norwich Union on the left.

The south bank of the Thames behind Vastern Road. Later in this book is recorded the redevelopment of this area.

Building of a footbridge over the Inner Distribution Road in Coley.

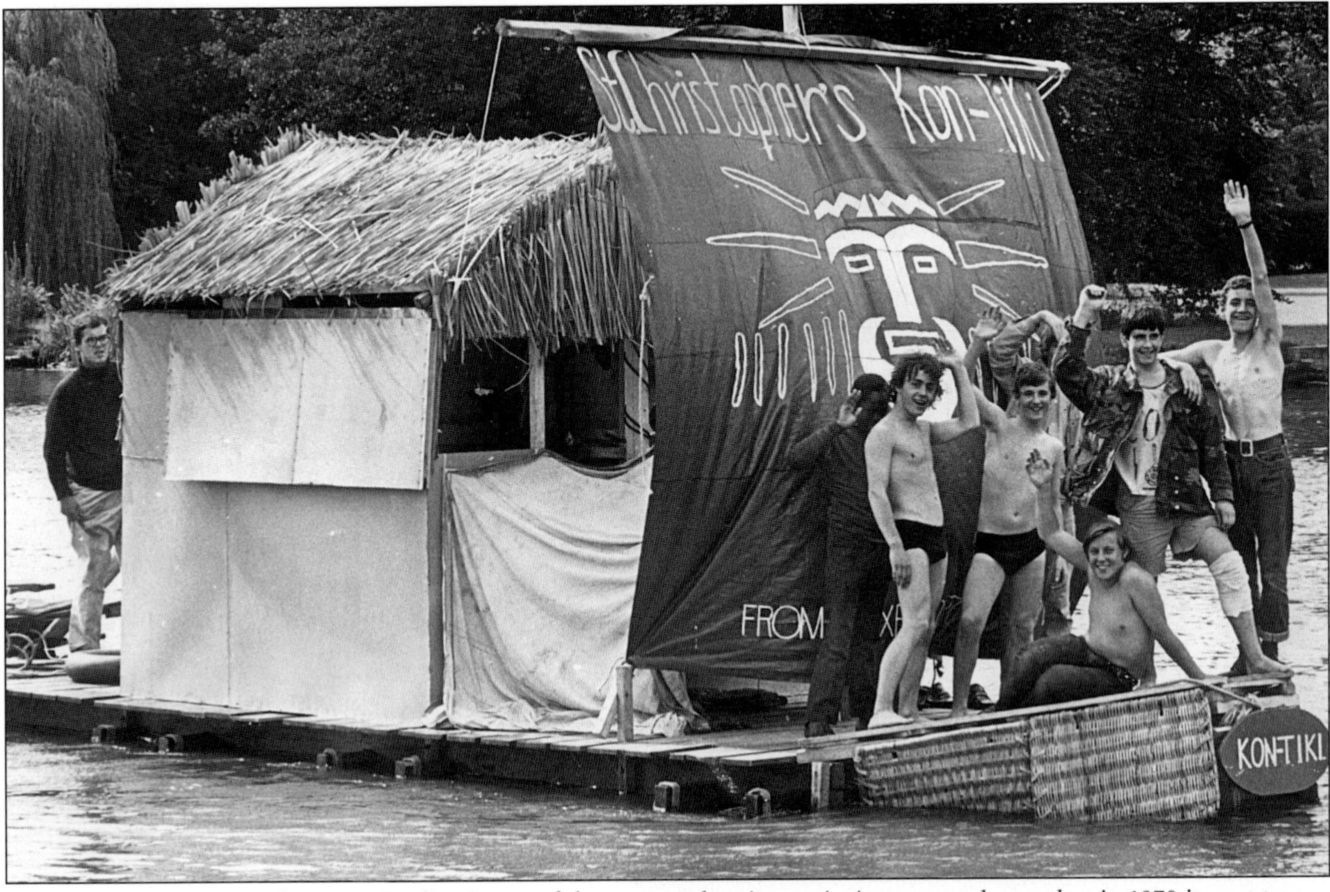

The stretch of the River Thames at Reading is one of the most enchanting on its journey to the sea, but in 1970 it saw strange craft as a group of young people built and sailed their own vessel.

Can anyone remember the days when the British Railways gave something away? Well to jog the memory, here is a picture of Sue Wright outside Reading station in November 1970, giving away 5s (25p) vouchers to people travelling from Reading to Paddington.

This young lady purchases a platform ticket which cost 2d (less than 1p). It allowed entry to the platform only.

No matter what the year or the decade, the attraction of Morris Dancing is always popular in both towns and villages. These Morris Dancers are entertaining the people at a Tilehurst Fete in 1970.

Time for merriment as people watch Morris Men dancing in the Forbury Gardens.

In the 1970s, Reading always looked forward to the twice-yearly visit of Traylen's Funfair.

Bridge Street with the completed flyover of the IDR and St Giles Church in the background.

The rebuilding of Brunel's Shepherd's House Bridge to accommodate the amount of traffic in the 1970s.

At the junction of London Street and Queen's Road, now part of the IDR, stood The English Leather Co., now a casino.

The Butts Shopping Centre in 1973, when people were asked not to buy Nescafé coffee because the manufacturers were importing it from Angola, which then had a reputation for exploiting cheap labour.

Kendrick Grammar School for Girls in London Road. This school has altered little from the outside.

Reading gaol, famous for inmate Oscar Wilde, was partly demolished in the 1970s and rebuilt to accommodate more prisoners.

The decade of the 1970s were years that many of us prefer to forget; there were power cuts, strikes, protests and demonstrations. It was in 1972 that it was decided to introduce plastic milk bottle. Here is a group of protesters with a huge mound of empty plastic milk bottles. Re-cycling of plastic was almost unheard of in those days.

After the Christmas celebrations in 1972 there was a pretty grim time for the residents of Reading because of a strike by the refuse collectors as piles of rubbish mounted up on the pavements.

The 1970s saw the full completion of the Inner Distribution Road (IDR). This aerial view shows the junction with Cheapside Centre, Greyfriars' Church on the left; to the far right is Oxford Road.

Aerial view with the Prudential building in the background, Shire Hall and Reading gaol in front it. Huntley & Palmers is in the foreground, and top right is the new Metal Box office.

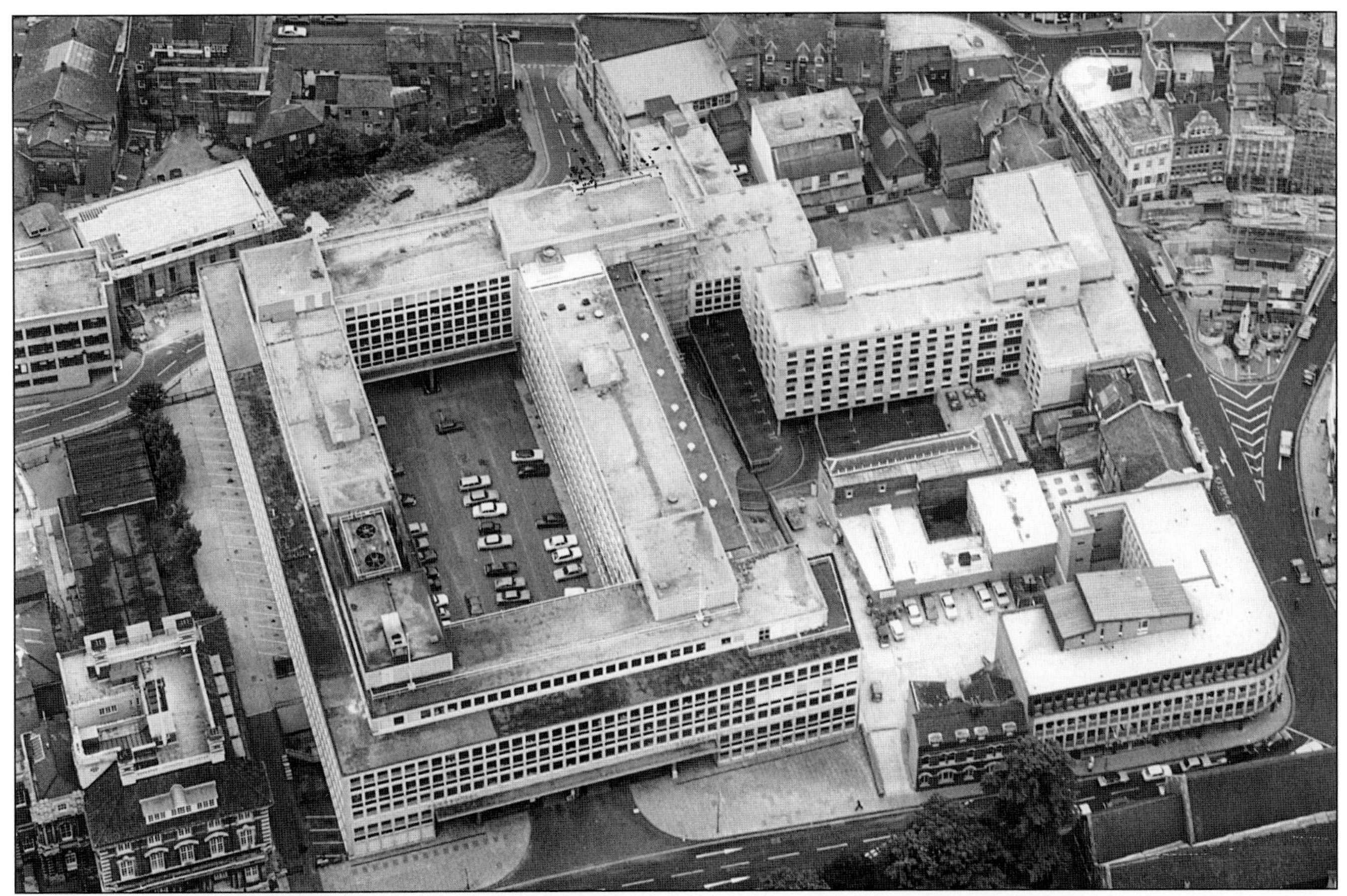

Part of this Prudential building was built on stilts, as originally the IDR was planned to go underneath it.

The wide open spaces of Bridge Street after the demolition of Simonds Brewery.

On 6 November 1973, on a cold, foggy evening, a 42-wagon freight train ploughed into an electrical relay station near Twyford. Two main lines were blocked and communications were totally lost on a seven-mile stretch of the line. But the accident might have been a lot more serious.

An ordinary passenger diesel and the experimental APT (Advanced Passenger Train).

The old iron-built Oxford Road railway bridge in the 1970s.

It was a worrying time for firemen when this petrol train, carrying 162,000 gallons of high-octane fuel, was derailed at Theale just outside Reading in 1974.

Alfred Sutton Girls' School in Wokingham Road.

July 1974 saw Reading's first female street sweeper. Here the first Lady of the Broom starts out on her rounds in Caversham.

In the 1970s, after the main body of soldiers had moved out of Brock Barracks, it was used for training young men and boys into the military service. Here, the Marines cadets are being inspected by the Southern Command Area Officer, Comm V.R. Lentaign.

Battle of Britain commemorations have always played a large part in Reading. This one in September 1974 marches past before the Mayor of Reading, Councillor Joe Bristow, at the Town Hall, Blargrave Street.

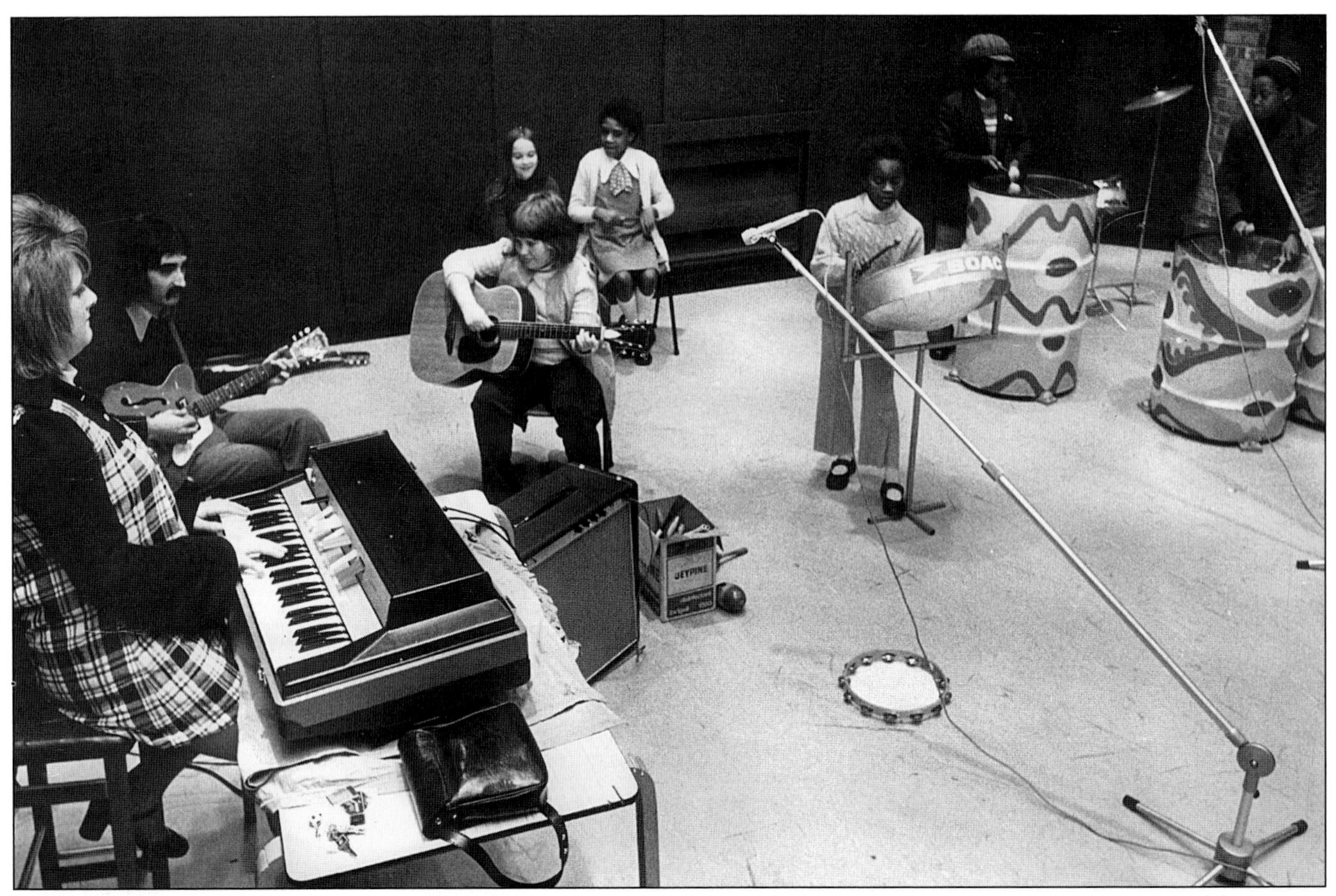

Having been a multi-cultural society for so many years, Reading has always found music high on the agenda. Here is the Oxford Road steel band at practice.

In January 1974 it was back to school for children all over Berkshire, but there was a consolation. In this picture, children from E.P. Collier School take part in a games lesson of snowballs at the Thameside Promenade.

Thirty years ago many of the Victorian schools in Reading had received little attention to improve their facilities. Some modernisation had taken place such as central heating, but here children were learning under very bad lighting conditions.

Happiness on the faces of these children from the Daphne Bennet School of Dancing, although their display nearly never took place as they had to be moved from the Willink School at Burghfield to St John's Hall at Mortimer in January 1974 because of an energy crisis and regular power cuts.

Children of Thameside School after their performance of *Snow White and the Seven Dwarfs.*

Today, children's school trips take them all over Europe and beyond, but 30 or 40 years ago it was a different story. These children from the Meadway School, Reading, are setting off on an expedition to the canals of Leicestershire.

Youth on the march! The young people of the Reading Youth Orchestra preparing to depart for Düsseldorf, Reading's twin town. The 92 members of the orchestra each paid £40 towards the tour, the balance coming from the orchestra's own funds.

These angelic faces belong to children singing *Sleep in Heavenly Peace* when performing in a Christmas nativity play at Earley.

Every year since the end of World War Two it had been traditional each Christmas to sing carols on the steps of the Royal Berkshire Hospital. Nurses and staff singing carols at Christmas 1970.

In the 1970s, the Top Rank ballroom on Station Hill in Reading was packed on a Saturday night. Here is one man who was particularly popular with the crowd, 'Barmy Steve Haines' and his disco.

Rock 'n' roll in the Top Rank ballroom on Station Hill.

The Brian Willmott School of Dancing was popular with people of all ages throughout Reading. This medals presentation dance was held at St Laurence's Hall, Abbey Square, Reading.

Members of the Sonning Girls' Choir on the stage at the old Town Hall, Reading, at a civic carol concert presented by Reading Salvation Army. The funds raised helped handicapped children.

These are members of the Woodley Old Tyme Dancing Club pose for the camera.

For many years up until the late 1970s, Reading had a very large naval land base at HMS *Dauntless*. It was the main training base for the Wrens and was located at Burghfield Common, just outside Reading. Here, Princess Anne, the Commandant of the WRENS, attends a passing-out inspection.

It was exceptionally hot during the summer of 1976 and one of the areas that had to be patrolled regularly was Highwood and South Lake. Here a local resident makes sure a fire lit by children was well and truly extinguished.

In 1975 part of Caversham Road caved into the Vastern Brook which flowed underneath.

The Mayor of Reading officially opening Fire Safety Week at the Butts Centre in the town.

Passengers travelling on the Penzance-Paddington train on 2 June 1976 had a narrow escape as the train was approaching Reading station. It had slowed for signals and was only travelling at about 15 miles when it jumped off the lines. Thankfully, nobody was injured.

There could have been a major disaster in Reading in 1977 when a train carrying bitumen came off the rails at Southcote Junction. One of the wagons collided with a gas cylinder which exploded. The cylinder was kept beside the tracks for use in stopping the points from freezing. Thanks to prompt action, a disaster was averted.

Manor Junior School in Ashampstead Road, Southcote, was built in the 1950s for the estate to cope with the new young families in the area. It is pictured here in the 1970s.

Schoolchildren in the Reading area have always played a prominent part in raising money for local charities. Here are children from Meadway Lower School, on a sponsored walk along the Thames, seen here passing the old Reading boathouse.

Orts Road, known as Newtown, was built for the workers of Huntley & Palmers and fell into a state of disrepair but has since been rebuilt.

A rather special event took place at Reading station in March 1978 when the commanding officer of HMS *Dauntless* unveiled this Class 50 locomotive named after the local naval land base.

How technology has changed. Stage and screen star Alfie Bass being shown the new Ticketron machine for issuing tickets at speed in Reading station.

An Inter-City 125 high-speed train zooms through Sonning Cutting, near Reading. Linking Reading with London, Bristol and South Wales, it travelled at speeds of up to 125mph, hence its name.

Reading was in the forefront of twinning with another town or city when it joined up with Düsseldorf in 1977. This picture shows celebrations in the market place.

Just about seven miles outside Reading is the Child Beale Trust and Nature Reserve. Here, members of the League of Friends accompany disabled people for a walk in the grounds.

This hospital fête in 1973 was opened by newsreader Michael Barrett who had recently been a patient in Battle Hospital.

One of the main attractions at hospital fêtes over the years was the Punch and Judy show. In the 1970s it was still going strong.

Over the last 35 years Reading has suffered various land subsidence; even in the year 2000 a road was cut off because of this. This picture takes us back to 1975, to Kentwood Close, Tilehurst, when residents suddenly found their back gardens had collapsed.

A march by students from Reading Labour Party, to the Houses of Parliament to protest about high unemployment figures in the 1970s.

A protest by NUPE (National Union of Public Employees) about large cuts in the National Health Service.

The right to work was a big issue in the 1970s. This is a demonstration by NUPE members.

By 1978 the country's power crisis was over and Christmas and New Year parties were well under way. This party, given by the 1st Emmer Green Guides, had as its guest 93-year-old Mrs Anne Warren.

A tiny child looks up into the face of Father Christmas as she offers him a plate of 'goodies' at the 1978 Christmas party for the children of Huntley & Palmers Social Club.

Christmas comes but once a year, and like most towns it is a big event in Reading.

In 1978 it was no exception, although Santa Claus arrived under clear blue skies as Reading enjoyed an Indian summer and Santa had turned up as early as October. The procession was led by the band of the RAMC from Aldershot.

A sea of smiling faces as children from the Oxford Road School rejoice at the Central Swimming Pool having just been presented with a cheque from the Courage brewery on being the winners of a swimming competition.

In 1978 these four strong lads were pushing a hospital bed from Reading to Maidenhead to raise money for Battle Hospital.

The 1970s saw many strikes. One of the most worrying, which lasted for nine weeks, was by local firemen. Service personnel drove wartime fire engines known as 'Green Goddesses' and no serious incidents occurred in the town.

When a craze hits young people there is no way of knowing to what lengths they will go to. But this was all in a good cause, to raise money for the Year of the Disabled.

Reading has always had an excellent Fire Service, who have had to deal with all manner of situations. This picture shows members of the brigade damping down a burnt-out motor launch on the River Thames.

In January 1979, at Whitley in Reading, this private house caught fire. The owner, despite suffering burns himself, managed to rescue the rest of the family.

February 1979 saw one of the largest fires in the centre of Reading for many years, when the furniture store of Waring Gillow was completely destroyed. This large furniture store extended through two streets, from Friar Street to Broad Street, and the entire building was gutted. Here crowds watch the fire.

Waring Gillow, completely destroyed and just a shell, was later rebuilt to become Littlewoods store.

The year of 1979 was a bad one in Reading when it came to fires. In April of that year an exclusive kitchen shop in Gun Street was wrecked in a spectacular blaze that took 50 firemen to bring under control.

Not surprisingly, even the good old fish and chip shops in Reading were not exempt from the many fires that took place that year. This fish and chip shop in Oxford Road was completely gutted.

In a busy town like Reading the firemen are called to all manner of different fires. Here they are attending a fire in a computer room in Reading.

In September 1979 there was another large fire in Reading, this time at one of the town's largest garages, Gowrings. Quick-thinking firemen and staff managed to get many of the cars out and away to safety.

It is always a sad day for many people when a popular milkman says a sad farewell. John Williams served his customers faithfully for 16 years.

In 1979, schoolteacher Chris Bertrand could stand the frustration of the classroom no longer and became a milkman instead. He said that not only was it quieter and healthier, the money was also much better!

Shire Hall

In 1975 a project was undertaken by Reading Borough Council to build Shire Hall at Shinfield Park for Berkshire County Council, whose offices were spread far and wide and needed to be housed all in one place. Plans were drawn up for the enormous development of what was to be known as the New Shire Hall complex.

A look at the new site in Shinfield Park for the construction of Shire Hall.

The beautiful Shinfield Park before the bulldozers moved in.

An aerial view of the half-built Shire Hall.

Shire Hall looking out over the M4 motorway.

Architect's model of the proposed building for Shire Hall, for many years the home of Berkshire County Council. Berkshire CC has since been dissolved and the building is now home to the Foster Wheeler group.

The ladies of the Shire Hall switchboard in 1975.

The 1980s

The 1960s and 1970s saw major alterations in Reading and the wholesale destruction of many areas with the building of the Inner Distribution Road. Huge amounts of earth had to be moved in order to take the traffic under Oxford Road. A flyover had to be built over Mill Lane which caused a major upheaval.

In contrast, the 1980s was a relatively quiet time because very little building work took place except to consolidate businesses. Just outside Reading, though, the A329M opened from the A4 Sutton Trial Ground through to Bracknell and Ascot. This gave huge relief to traffic in the town.

The Mayor of Reading in 1980 was Councillor Marion Absolom and here she is with a group of happy schoolchildren from E.P. Collier School who are taking a book they have prepared to present to the children at a school in Barbados.

Hospital fêtes in Reading have always been very successful, well-organised and with record crowds attending them. Here, the late and much-loved Roy Castle is opening the fête in the grounds of Battle Hospital. These have now been going for 42 years.

Pupils of Oxford Road Primary School wave goodbye to lessons on a day in July 1980. They are off on a day trip to Windsor Safari Park, which has now become Legoland.

The protests of the 1970s spilled over into the 1980s when the Conservative Government was considering closing down some comprehensive schools.

One of the largest car dealers in Reading over the past 70 years was Vincent's, with its showroom in Station Square. In 1982 Vincent's still retained this small showroom in Castle Street.

It is always nice to see the Army drop in when there is a school fête on, especially when they are from the Red Devils parachute team. Here they are at a fête in Tilehurst in 1983.

The high-flying skills of the Army Junior Gymnastics Team at Westwood School fête thrilled the crowds and the pupils with their impressive demonstration which helped to raise £1,700 for school funds.

Veterans step out to mark the 40th anniversary of the end of World War Two. This parade took place in 1985 when 400 old soldiers and airmen marched down Oxford Road to Brock Barracks. The parade was led by the band of the 2nd Wessex Regiment and contained Dunkirk veterans and men from the Burma Star Association.

It seems impossible now, looking at this picture, that this was the scene at the junction of King's Road and Queen's Road in 1986, but in the top right-hand corner you can see the builders already at work developing this area.

In the 1980s, many people fought to save the famous building called the Mansion House which stands in Prospect Park and was once the home of the Kendrick family. This is Mr Mellnick, who started the campaign to raise £1 million to save this historic building. He was in his 90s when this picture was taken . He would be pleased to see that the Mansion House has been saved and is now a restaurant.

'Stop playing politics with the Playschemes,' the banner reads in 1986.

Right in the centre of town outside the Civic Offices is this very fine sculpture called 'The Wall', a tribute to the youth of Reading. This picture shows its unveiling in April 1981 by Herr Burgermeister Klaus Bungert from Düsseldorf, Reading's twin town. With him is Councillor Marion Absolom and chief executive Harry Tee.

By the 1980s, Burghfield Mill, one mile from Southcote, had been allowed to fall into a state of disrepair. Later in the book you will see this is now a magnificent block of flats.

The bus depot in Mill Lane will bring back happy memories to those who worked there. It has been completely demolished and part of The Oracle shopping centre now stands on the site.

An aerial view of old Reading and new Reading. In the bottom left-hand corner stands the Western Tower offices beside the railway station. The dark building is the Foster Wheeler offices and in the top left-hand corner is the old and new prison. To the right is Caversham.

The 1990s

The old railway station, built in the time of Brunel, is a Reading landmark. It is now the Three Guineas public house.

Station Square is dominated by a statue of Edward VII, looking up Station Road towards Queen Victoria Street.

Looking from St Laurence's Church, the imposing figure of Queen Victoria looks towards Reading railway station.

The Old Market Place has now been modernised. On the left is the entrance to the Corn Exchange and in the centre the now-closed public toilets.

The relocated Post Office in the Market Place and further down to the right the modern building which replaced Sutton Seeds shop.

Crossroads at Jackson's Corner, now dominated by the Abbey National and looking towards Duke Street Bridge.

Jackson's Corner with the still privately-owned Jackson's department store.

Old Duke Street Bridge. The original was built three centuries ago to take the barges up the river to the original Oracle factory.

In the heart of Reading are the beautiful Forbury Gardens with a Victorian bandstand just a few yards from the Maiwand Lion which commemorates that famous Afghanistan battle.

A more modern war memorial at the entrance to Forbury Gardens to commemorate those who died in the wars this century.

Fountain and fishpond in Forbury Gardens with St James's RC Church in the centre and the original war memorial to the right.

Modernisation of some of the older buildings in the Oxford Road. This one was the old McIlroy's department store which is now split into smaller shop units.

The Butts Shopping Centre, built in 1970, is now called Broad Street Mall and is about to be developed yet again.

Modernised shops and offices in Oxford Road, opposite Broad Street Mall.

The busy corner of Oxford Road and West Street, developed over the years to replace the Maypole Dairy and Marks & Spencer.

Langstons, the well-known clothing store on the corner of West Street which is now Shipley's amusement arcade.

It is important to feature Greyfriars, one of the leading churches in the centre of Reading. This ancient church was once an open prison.

Looking down Friar Street to the Town Hall, on the left with its large columns is the now boarded-up ABC Cinema. What will happen to this building in the near future?

St Mary's Butts and the Minster Church of St Mary the Virgin.

Looking up King's Road to the rebuilding of Debenhams in preparation to become an entrance to The Oracle.

In the late 1990s there were massive alterations now taking place in Broad Street as shops and buildings were altered to fit in with the new entrance to The Oracle shopping centre.

An early-morning view of the roof tops of Reading, from Broad Street Mall car park. The skyline is dominated by the building of The Oracle and in the distance is the spire of St Giles's Church.

An ancient part of Reading was destroyed to build this glass office block on the corner of Crane Wharf and King's Road.

One of the finest pieces of architecture completed in the 1980s was the Prudential building on the site of the old Huntley & Palmers factory.

The very busy Cemetery Junction which has changed very little over the years.

Wycliffe Baptist Church with the Arthur Hill swimming pool and public baths next door.

The newly-modernised Granby public house, originally called the Marquis of Granby, at Cemetery Junction.

Wokingham Road is one of Reading's busiest roads.

A well-known landmark is the Three Tuns public house at the junction of Wokingham Road and Church Road. Until the turn of the century, the original Three Tuns stood on the opposite side of the road.

One of the most famous streets in Reading is London Street. The building on the left, with the large pillars, was built for the Institute of Civil Engineering. It later became a chapel and then the Everyman Theatre. It is now the Great Expectations public house.

The spire of Christ Church in the distance and on the right is the recently-installed replica of the Whitley Pump where cattle were watered in the old days.

The newly-restored Mansion House, which is now a restaurant.

View from the Mansion House across Prospect Park. The beacon is lit on special occasions.

Caversham Bridge was one of the first pre-cast concrete bridges. To test its strength before it was opened, 38 traction engines were driven on to it at the same time.

The gateway to Battle Hospital, which will be preserved when the rest of the hospital is pulled down and redeveloped.

Here is an unusual sight for the town of Reading, when two mounted officers from Thames Valley Police patrolled through St Mary's Butts on a Saturday afternoon.

When this building was put up 35 years ago as the headquarters for Thames Water, it was said to be one of the most modern buildings in the town. It has now been pulled down and replaced by a circular office block which you will see later in the book.

This side street in Reading, known as Cheapside, was once the main entertainment centre of the town. Here is the now-closed down Odeon Cinema. Next to that, where the block of offices now stands, was once the Palace Theatre.

Further up Broad Street, we see this once busy thoroughfare for cars and buses now turned into a very enjoyable, traffic-free shopping area.

In Friar Street we stop to look at the old Tudor Tavern, surrounded by the many small shops which go to make this street.

One of the very busy junctions in Reading, at the junction of Friar Street and Cheapside, this used to be known as 'Co-op Corner', but as you can see the Co-op has closed down and it is now a Primark department store.

The Oracle

With the building of The Oracle shopping centre in the 1990s came the largest development in Reading for a century. Before then the industrial turning point for Reading was from 1800 to the mid-1930s with the commercial ventures of Simonds Brewery, Huntley & Palmers and Sutton's Seeds. It is fair to say that these three businesses were responsible for the growth of Reading, together with the retail development that came with the building of A.H. Bull, Mcllroy's, Heelas, Wellsteed's, the Co-op and Messrs Jackson's of Jackson's Corner department store.

The next part of the book will be devoted to this growth of Reading, starting with The Oracle shopping centre.

The foundations of The Oracle between Bridge Street, London Street and Minster Street in 1998. Courage Brewery had already moved its factory from this site to Worton Grange.

The footings being prepared for the building of the multi-screen cinema in The Oracle.

A good view of the start of the massive multi-storey car park and in the background we see the Inner Distribution Road and St Giles's Church.

The skyline is a mass of huge cranes and the footings and foundations in the centre show the pillars for the car park. The main shopping centre, in the middle, is already under way.

This view of 80ft-high cranes constructing the pillars for the car park is amazing.

A beautiful view of the Kennet as it flows through the early construction of The Oracle.

During construction of this massive operation, huge queues of traffic formed, sometimes stretching a mile back to Caversham.

The complicated and enormous framework of the Warner Bros multi-screen cinema.

The shopping area being built beside the River Kennet.

The intricate and very detailed nature of building a car park on such a vast scale.

The main structure of the new Debenhams store beside the Kennet.

The Oracle nearing completion. In the centre is the car park; on the right, the roof is about to be put on the cinema. Later, you will see the completed Oracle shopping centre.

The Year 2000

An evening view of Blagrave Street from the railway station. In the distance is the Town Hall.

One of the largest roundabouts in Reading is the Forbury roundabout. Silhouetted in the background can be seen the Thames Water buildings.

One of the beauties of The Oracle shopping centre is the many waterside cafés and restaurants as seen in this picture.

The Oracle shopping centre is so vast that it has room to house a visit from a 'Batmobile' type of car.

Looking down Greyfriars Road to the bottom of Station Hill, we now see a street lined with large offices where once stood rows of terraced houses and small shops.

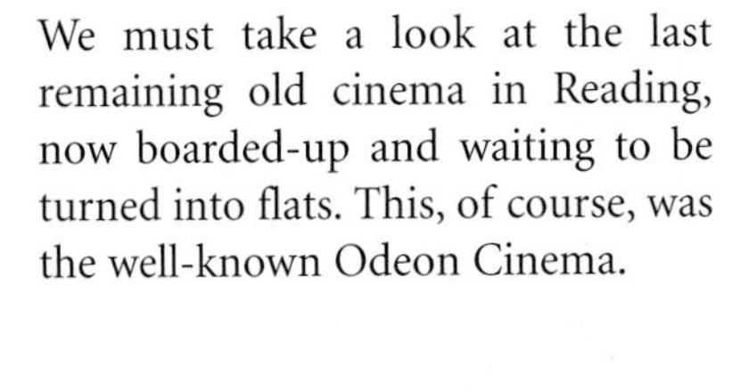

We must take a look at the last remaining old cinema in Reading, now boarded-up and waiting to be turned into flats. This, of course, was the well-known Odeon Cinema.

The Warner Village multi-screen cinema in The Oracle was bound to cause the demise of the small cinemas.

It is understandable that The Oracle Shopping Centre with the River Kennet running through it should have seen its fair proportion of floods.

We see this brilliant picture looking across the River Kennet to the King's Road, capturing the sunlight reflecting on the sides of the large office blocks.

Into 2001

IT is now the month of September 2001 and as I write this book I reflect on the vast changes that have happened in our town of Reading over the last 11 years and in this penultimate chapter we look at some of the ultra-modern buildings around the borough of Reading.

We have looked at the building of the Shire Hall complex at Shinfield Park in the 1970s and we have dealt at length with the construction of The Oracle Shopping Centre. At the end of the book we will look at the magnificent Madejski Stadium with its hotel and leisure complex.

Now I am going to take you on a picture tour of some of the other smaller but equally important new buildings that have sprung up all over the borough of Reading, in particular the Vastern Road area where, in my opinion, there are some of the finest office blocks in the town; in fact, I would call them architectural perfection.

We also travel out to look at the buildings on the Sutton's trading estate on the main A4 London Road and as you go out of the town there is another group of buildings known as the Oracle development. In this complex there is a fitness centre for use by the hundreds of workers employed in the area.

I think it is right to say that Reading is now one of the leading towns in the South of England and I am proud to be part of it. Maybe in the future we can look forward to the City of Reading.

One of the first business parks to be completed in the 1990s was the Arlington Business Park in Theale.

The Showcase Cinema complex at Winnersh.

Part of the huge Computer Centre in Green Park. When it is completed, 5,000 staff will be employed there.

The delightful walk through The Oracle shopping centre.

A three-way view of the old and new at the bottom of Southampton Street. On the left, two century-old cottages; in the centre the Inner Distribution Road; and in the background the new office block completed in the 1990s.

The beauty of St Saviour's Church and Drop-in Centre, not far from The Oracle. Not a new building but still serving the people of Reading.

Opposite St Saviour's Church in Berkeley Avenue is a new housing development on land which previously housed the Thames Water headquarters.

The junction of King Street and Broad Street shows the main entrance to The Oracle (see right archway). The building above Coffee Republic was, three centuries ago, the home of Lord Walsingham and has since been restored to its original splendour.

A close-up of the arched entrance to The Oracle.

Luxury flats being built on the site of Reading's best known cinema, The Rex.

West Street was once a street of many small shops. Primark is on the right and the remains of the brick-built entrance to Palmer Hall used in the 20th century for concerts and plays.

Field Road, where old and new houses stand on old chalk mines which have since caved in. Work is in progress to restore these houses.

The road bridge over the River Kennet at Berkeley Avenue, only half a mile from the town centre.

A mixture of the old Abbey walls together with a modern sculpture in the centre of the town.

Abbey Gateway contrasting against the modern buildings.

From the River Kennet and Crane Wharf NatWest Bank House.

An interesting scene of the King's Road Bridge, nestled between the trees where once stood the famous 'shop on the bridge' and now stands a new public house.

Flats on the Kennet Side at the junction of Watlington Street and King's Road.

Part of the old Huntley & Palmers biscuit factory now turned into flats after many heated discussions about its demolition. On the left the Prudential building.

Reading Prison pictured from the River Kennet standing on Gasworks Bridge.

Blake's Lock from Gas Works Road.

From the rear of the Prudential we see the new bridge and island specially built to bring charm to the area.

Parts of old Reading with the Kennet Side from Forbury Road.

Along from the prison is the Energis building, built 30 years ago as the head office for Metal Box. In the coming months this will be demolished.

The unchanging scene of the Forbury Gardens, the beautiful area in the centre of Reading with the new Law Courts in the background.

On the right is the Apex Plaza, built in pink and white marble. In the centre, opposite the station, is the old Foster Wheeler building, now called Thames Tower.

The charming Rising Sun pub, dwarfed in the land of giant offices.

The new Thames Water headquarters built on the banks of the River Thames.

Thames Water from Christchurch Meadows, on the opposite side of the River Thames.

Reading Bridge from Hill's Meadow, dwarfed by the Thames Water building.

The Thames towpath towards Caversham Lock.

The magnificent flats behind Vastern Road on the River Thames. Rows of terraced houses were pulled down to build these.

At the top of Vastern Road, and fronting the luxury riverside flats, are the new office block and conference centre, Great Brighams Mead.

Caversham Bridge and Piper's Island taken from Fry's Island.

The rear of the Crown Court, standing just yards from the Abbey Gateway.

Green Park where the ITC dwarfs this tiny preserved timbered cottage.

For many years an empty water tower stood at Tilehurst. Here it is being converted into flats.

Station Hill.

At the bottom of Station Hill, boarded up cottages are waiting for demolition.

The now closed Duke of Edinburgh public house next to RG1 nightclub.

To slow down the flow of traffic through Southcote Estate, there are bollards which rise from the road in rush hour.

Entrance of the Mecca Bingo Hall, Station Hill.

Station Hill and taxi ranks with the new railway station in the background.

The Courage Brewery at Worton Grange.

Health and fitness centre at Earley, used by office staff from the Sutton's Business Park.

The Brunel Railway Bridge in Newtown with the footbridge in the distance.

The new footbridge built to span the River Kennet for the new housing development in Gas Works Road.

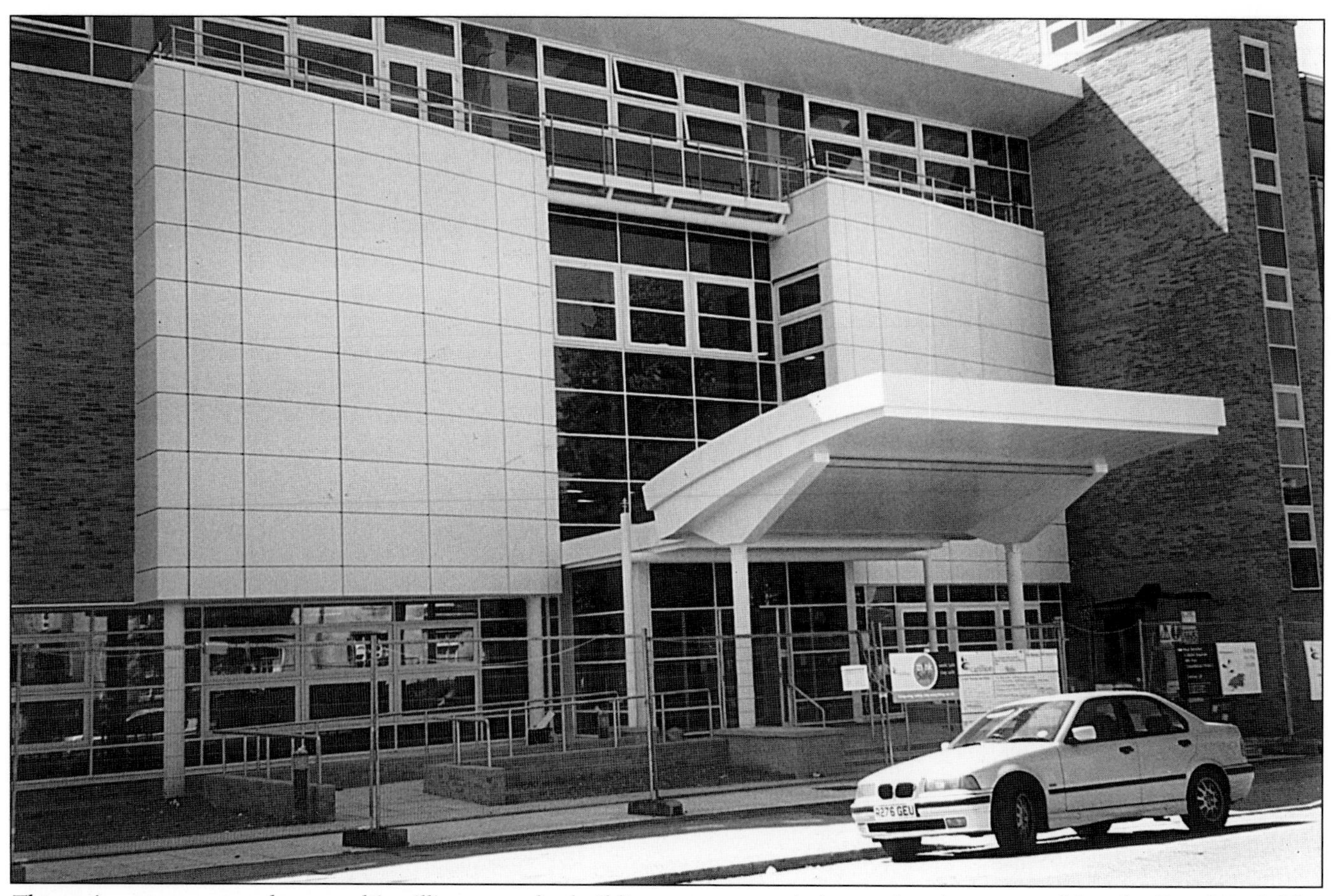

The main entrance to a huge multi-million pound rebuilding programme being undertaken to combine the Royal Berkshire Hospital and Battle Hospitals.

Further development next to the Turk's Head public house on the London Road towards the town centre where Café Ole used to be. The Turk's Head, now called the Fez and Firkin, is still frequented by the nearby student brigade.

The flats at Coley Park Estate.

The Red Cow at the junction of London Road and Southampton Street.

The old railway arches are put to good use on Caversham Road and Abattoir Road as they have now been converted to house Reading Jazz Club.

The fire station in Caversham Road was built in the 1950s and is still in use.

One of the oldest transport cafés in Reading is Stewart's Café in Woodley, opened well over 50 years ago.

The redundant Woodley police station, across the road from Stewart's Café.

The aviation museum in Woodley, just outside Reading.

The drinking fountain which has stood on this site outside St Laurence's Church for centuries, was put there for travellers on the road.

St Mary's Church has stood for over 1,000 years. Parts of this church were built with stones from the old Reading Abbey.

In the town centre there is a comparison of the old and the new with the Tudor-style houses contrasting with the cold concrete buildings of Broad Street Mall. Pavlov's Dog, now an eatery, was once the home of one of the first shops to sell radios and televisions in Reading. Next door but one used to be the headquarters of the Salvation Army.

In the old part of Reading we look at one of the narrowest and most famous streets in the town. Its official name is Union Street but it is known locally as Smelly Alley, the reason being that for the first half of the last century most of the shops were either fishmongers, butchers or greengrocers. As can be seen from the signs, this has all altered.

We leave Smelly Alley and travel across the road to another narrow street known as Merchants' Place. Here you see the old stables and living quarters for the coachmen, now turned into antique and collectors' shops.

If you come back out of Merchants' Place into Friar Street, you emerge beside the old ABC Cinema and the now unused Boar's Head pub. All this area is due for redevelopment.

Reading's town centre used to comprise many streets and alleyways. This narrow street, known as Cross Street, once housed many small shops and businesses.

Just a few yards along from Cross Street is Queen Victoria Street, once considered one of the most exclusive and expensive streets in Reading. The upper architecture is extremely interesting, built in Victorian times just a few hundred yards from Brunel's Reading railway station.

This is a perfect picture of the far end of Friar Street with an entrance to the large Town Hall and St Laurence's Church. Its charm is enhanced by the trees and other greenery planted over the last ten years.

Our journey through Reading, past the Town Hall and church takes us into the old Market Place, now much modernised.

Over King Street traffic lights is the old Duke Street. This street used to be made up of dozens of shops. On the right-hand side is the old Ship Inn, well known to the stagecoach travellers.

Around the corner form Duke Street is Marks & Spencer, slightly hidden by these newly-planted trees. Just before that is the entrance to Market Way.

A recent development in Friar Street, the street of many pubs, is The Walkabout Australian pub, seen here through an alleyway by the old General Post Office.

The ultra-modern, huge three-sided clock at the Civic Offices.

Leaving the town centre, travelling along Richfield Avenue, are the offices and production centre of Berkshire Press, the home of the *Evening Post* and many other newspapers.

On the opposite side of the road to the *Evening Post* is the largest leisure and sporting complex in the town, known as Rivermead Leisure Centre. It houses a large swimming pool, sporting arena and gymnasium. In the summer it is also the home to two major entertainment events, one being the famous WOMAD (World of Music and Dance) the other the long-standing Reading Festival, which together attract 100,000 people.

Beside Richfield Avenue, on the journey to Caversham, flows the beautiful River Thames. Here is the view looking across it to the recently-built restaurant and pub, Chronicles.

This panoramic view taken by photographer Michael Hill, standing on Caversham Bridge, shows the vast expanse and charm of the River Thames at Reading. It also shows the large amount of riverside building of luxury flats that has taken place over the past ten years or so. On the extreme left is Piper's Island.

This enchanting view is of Piper's Island, one of the few remaining islands in the centre of the Thames, just close to Caversham Bridge. On this tiny island is a restaurant and pub.

These river boats take you upstream from Piper's Island (opposite side to the previous photograph) to Mapledurham House and the old mill.

Looking from the other side of Caversham Bridge, we see the Reading Rowing Club boathouse. This was built 20 years ago to replace some of the very old boathouses that used to hire out rowing boats and punts.

If you stroll down the lane beside the boathouse to the towpath you will come across this enchanting scene of swans and pigeons. In the centre of the traffic island stands a drinking fountain erected by the will of Mrs S.G. Attwells in memory of her husband Frank, Mayor of Reading 1891-92, who died during his term of office.

Just across the road from the drinking fountain is the newly-built Holiday Inn. The main bar is called the *Three Men in a Boat*, after the book by Jerome K. Jerome. The three men in the boat moored here and stayed at the old Caversham Bridge Hotel on their journey down the River Thames.

This excellent view of Caversham Bridge from Thameside Promenade shows the ferro-concrete bridge built in 1928.

This view taken from the Thames shows the parish church of St Peter's and the grounds of Caversham Court. In 1799, William Simonds, of the famous firm of brewers in Reading, leased the riverside mansion of Caversham Court. Always with an eye for business, he made good money from digging out chalk pits in the garden of his house. The Tudor house was demolished and replaced by one built by the famous architect Augustus Welby Pugin, itself to be demolished in 1933.

Travelling down the Thames from Caversham Bridge, we go past the exclusive riverbank houses known as The Warren. This view here is of the recently-built Canoe Club.

If we travel down the Thames towards Henley, we pass the war memorial for those men of Caversham who died in World Wars One and Two.

The village of Caversham and the century-old public library. Next to it now stands the New Testament Church of God, once the well-loved Glendale Cinema.

Further down the river we see two more of the town's boat houses.

Most of the village of Caversham has changed little with the passage of time. The Spice Oven Restaurant was once the home of Baylis, the well-known family grocers which traded there for nearly 70 years.

The main shopping street, known as Prospect Street, is now a very busy road but it still remains a street of small shopkeepers.

To get in and out of Caversham from Reading you have to travel over one of the two bridges. Here we have a view leaving Caversham via Caversham Bridge.

Once over Caversham Bridge towards Reading, at the junction of Richfield Avenue, on the right is the Gorge Café, well-known in the area for its large breakfasts.

Here is one of the largest car dealers in Reading, standing on a site used for the sale of cars for well over 70 years. The original firm was Gowerings.

The Madejski Stadium

READING, like most towns and cities, has for the past 100 years boasted a flourishing football team. I am not going into the history of the Reading 'Royals' here, as it is well-documented in other books.

Instead, this final chapter is the story of one man's interest in the town's football club, from the 1990s to the present day. Local business man Mr John Madejski took the ailing club under his financial wing and pulled it round to see it playing its home games in one of the finest football grounds in Europe today.

The chairman of Reading FC and builder of the Madejski Stadium, John Madejski.

John Madejski cutting the first turf for the football pitch in 1997.

It was obvious from the earliest days of Mr Madejski's involvement that if the club were to get anywhere, then it would mean building a new stadium, as the old one at Elm Park, though much-loved, was too old and certainly not big enough if the ultimate dream of Premiership football was to be realised.

A new site was found on the old landfill site at Whitley. There were major complications but these were overcome and Reading FC now boasts the most magnificent stadium together with a major hotel and conference centre, offering all the amenities that anyone could desire. The stadium can seat over 24,000 people.

The 66-acre site was owned by Reading Borough Council and situated close to junction 11 of the M4. It was a landfill site and extensive work had to be carried out before construction could begin.

Soil and rubble which was moved to the car park area to create a 16-acre retail park which was sold to help fund the site.

Preparations for the football pitch itself.

After the football pitch was laid, work began on the stands.

A distant view of the many miles of steel work needed for the building of the stands.

A view of the pitch from the half-completed stands.

Spacious stadium seating specially designed to provide an unrestricted view of the pitch from every seat.

Nearly completed – a view of the stands.

The stadium and the Royals Conference Centre which has facilities for 750 people.

The hotel complex known as the Millennium Madejski Hotel.

Players and directors of Reading Football Club in 1948-49, when the club finished runners-up in the old Third Division South.

The Royals from 1970-71. Back row (left to right): Stuart Morgan, Barrie Wagstaff, Dennis Allen, Steve Death, Will Dixon, Dennis Butler, Fred Sharpe. Front row: Gordon Cumming, Terry Bell, Les Chapell, John Haley, Dick Habbin, Tony Wagstaff, Bobby Williams. At the end of the season the club was relegated to Division Four.

Reading FC, 1986-87. Back row (left to right): Gary Peters, Steve Wood, Bob Bassett, Martin Hicks, Gary Westwood, Trevor Senior, Paul Canoville. Middle: Glen Hunter (physiotherapist), Steve Head, Andy Rogers, Colin Baillie, Terry Hurlock, Brian Roberts, Jerry Williams, Dean Horrix. Front: Stuart Beavon, Mark White, Ian Branfoot (manager), Kevin Bremner, Steve Richardson. That season the Royals finished mid-table in the old Second Division, the equivalent of today's First Division.

Aerial view of Elm Park which was situated in a highly-populated area of Reading. There were few parking facilities and on match days Reading town centre often ground to a halt.

The Royals in action against Derby County at Elm Park in the 1990s.

The end of the season for the Royals before the move to the new stadium.

A capacity crowd for the lap of honour at the last match at Elm Park.

The housing estate that now stands on the site of Reading's Elm Park football ground.

Subscribers

Geoffrey Aburrow

Rosemary Andrew

Alan Barnes

B J Bartholomew

Lynda Billing

Neil Carpenter

Eric Davies

Mrs Sheila E Deacon

Rosemarie A Donaldson

Michael Earley

Paul Field

Mr & Mrs Anthony J Fish

Margaret Glancy

Charles L Goddard

Iris V Godding

D H Grainger

P Grainger

Ms G. Higgs

Mrs S Holt

Barbara Kirsop

Mr F Lawrence

Maggie Lawson

Robert Lee

Stephen Mead

R W Middleton

R M Millard

Win Povey

R W Sopp

Victor Stacey

Mrs E M Strange

Mr J K Turner

Mrs B Unwin

Mr Robert Unwin

Brian John Walker

Alfred Warrick

Paul A Welton

C Wootton